NO
UNCERTAIN
TERMS

NO UNCERTAIN TERMS

Mark Dittrick and Diane Kender Dittrick

Illustrations by Tom Bloom

Facts On File Publications
New York, New York ● Bicester, England

No Uncertain Terms

Library of Congress Cataloging in Publication Data

Dittrick, Mark.
  No Uncertain Terms.

  Includes index.
    1. Vocabulary.   2. English language—Errors of usage.
  3. English language—Glossaries, vocabularies, etc.   I. Dittrick,
  Diane Kender.   II. Title.
  PE1449.D57   1984   428.1   83-16631
  ISBN 0-87196-217-9 (pbk.)

Printed in the United States of America

For
John M. Dittrick
and
Norma Louise Morris

Contents

Foreword

Diane Kender Dittrick and Mark Dittrick want me to tell you that this is a *Foreword*—not a *Preface*. Authors themselves can write either of these for their own books, but the forewords to many books are now written by the authors' colleagues or friends. The authors then write their own preface. This would please Henry W. Fowler, who wrote in his still very useful and popular *Dictionary of Modern English Usage* (1926):

> "Foreword is a word invented . . . as a Saxonism by anti-latinists, and caught up as a vogue-word by the people who love a new name for an old thing. *Preface* has a 500-year history behind it in English, and, far from being antiquated, is still *the* name for the thing. It is to be hoped that the vogue may pass . . . A decent retirement might be found for *foreword* if it were confined to the particular kind of preface that is supplied by some distinguished person for a book written by someone else who feels the need of a sponsor."

I do not know that Fowler would consider me "distinguished," but I am happy to fill his and the Dittricks' desire that a foreword to a book be written by someone other than its author or authors.

Many authors, of course, do not follow Fowler's wishes and still choose to call their own preface a *foreword,* usually to imply that it is less formal, and shorter, than if they had called it a *preface.* Thus the University of Chicago Press's *Manual of Style,* while agreeing that a foreword is "a statement by someone other than the author" and a preface "the author's own statement," points out that, no matter who writes the foreword, it is normally no more than two to four pages long.

The authors certainly don't need a "sponsor," but what Mr. Fowler wanted and the authors needed was just someone's name other than their own at the end of this foreword. I am pleased to have been asked to contribute to this very entertaining book, and hope you will enjoy it as much as I did.

Stuart B. Flexner
Editor-in-Chief of The Random
House Dictionaries

Preface

What possessed us to write this book? Without whose help would the writing of it have been next to impossible? These are questions suitably answered in a preface—a short statement at the beginning of a book by the author or authors of the book *about* the book.

Our personal and professional interest in nailing down the names of things provided the major motivation for writing *No Uncertain Terms*. What also possessed us to write it, though, was our personal and professional possession of a key to an apartment in Manhattan, where rents nowadays are paid in megabucks.

Those individuals who helped in one big way or another include, in alphabetical order: George J. Billy, Laura Chunosoff; Sondra Cohen; Margo Dewhurst; Sarah Friend; Nat Grau; Jeremy Jackson; Kate Klimo; George Koppelman; David Lomax; Esther Mitgang; Kipp and Margo Osborne; Mark Petracca; Walter Rapawy; Peter Skinner; Capt. Albert Stwertka; and Fay Webern.

And a very special thanks to Ben Seitzman, a real mensch who deserves a real special mention for a measure of encouragement that made a measurable difference.

Introduction

What makes a spire a spire and not a steeple? A bug a bug and not a beetle? Why are you all wet if you think a pier is a kind of dock? Is a gorge nothing more than just a not-so-grand canyon? Would calling a monk a friar be a clerical error?

That's what *No Uncertain Terms* is all about: the seemingly simple names of things; words we all *think* we know; familiar terms even the brainiest individuals regularly confuse with other familiar, usually closely related terms; easy terms (not to be confused with tempting time payments) easily confused. The English language is chock-full of them. And so is *No Uncertain Terms*.

An introduction, by the way, unlike both a preface and a foreword, is usually considered part of a book's text and therefore frequently begins, as this one does, on page one. Unlike a preface, an introduction is a statement at the beginning of a book that is not about the book itself but about what the book is about. And, unlike a foreword, an introduction, like a preface, ought to be authored by a book's author or authors. (Just imagine how embarrassing it would have been if we had asked Stuart B. Flexner to write our introduction.)

A Dock, a Wharf,
A Pier

Whoever originally recommended a long walk on a short pier was surely up to no good, and also up on his marine-terminal terminology.

A DOCK:

Not a solid something at all, as most suppose, to take any sort of stroll on. A dock is *the area of water next to a wharf or pier.* The body of water, or basin, between two piers is also called a dock. A dock is what a boat or ship that's been docked is docked *in.* Wharves and piers are what runabouts, battleships, and love boats tie up *to.*

A WHARF:

Any structure that vessels tie up to that is *built along and parallel to the shore.*

A PIER:

Any structure that vessels tie up to that *runs out and away from,* and usually at a right angle to, *the shore.*

The wharf-pier distinction is even clearer when more technical port parlance is applied to the two: *marginal wharf* and *finger pier.* And when it comes to the latter, New York City is a port without peers, boasting 868 perpendicular docking digits at last count.

A Meteor,
A Meteorite,
A Meteoroid

Plunging brightly through the night,
Are you a meteoroid or a meteorite?
An "-ite" in the night?
An "-oid" in the void?
Or perhaps you're neither,
And only a meteor.

A METEOR:
This is the phenomenon commonly called a "shooting star," characterized by a bright streak of light produced when a particle (usually no bigger than a grain of sand) from space enters (at a speed somewhere between 80,000 and 216,000 miles per hour), plunges through, and is vaporized in the earth's atmosphere. A very large and particularly bright meteor is called a *fireball*. A fireball that explodes as it hurtles through the atmosphere is called a *bolide*.

A METEORITE:
A meteor that survives. Any fireball, bit of bolide, or other piece of interplanetary debris that makes it safely to terra firma has earned the right to be designated a meteorite. Meteorites also fall into categories: *siderites*, or *irons* (those made mostly of iron); *aerolites*, or *stones* (mostly of stone); and *siderolites* (a mixture of iron and stone). The largest known meteorite, a South African siderite, weighs close to 60 tons.

A METEOROID:
Any small particle still traveling through space in search of a suitable atmosphere to end it all in in a voidless blaze of -oidless glory, and perhaps go on to greater (maybe even crater) things.

A Bug, a Beetle

Ladybug, ladybug,
Fly away home.
Your house is on fire,
And your children are
misnomed.

A BUG:
As any entomologist worth his or her butterfly net knows, a ladybug, while it may or may not be a lady, is certainly no bug. Nor is a lightningbug (a.k.a. a firefly), any more than it's a fly. Both, along with a long list of similarly mischristened winged critters, are beetles. True bugs, of which there are well over 50,000 different species, belong to the insect order Hemiptera and differ from beetles in several dramatic ways.

Bugs suck, which is not a value judgment—except perhaps in the case of the bed bug, a true bug that truly sucks, lacking as it does the equipment to do what it has gotten such a rotten reputation for doing: biting.

Bug wings—the uppermost pair of two, that is—are normally thick at the base and thin and membranous at the tips, at which points they invariably overlap when at rest. A beetle's topmost wings are decidedly different.

And baby bugs and baby beetles develop into, respectively, big bugs and big beetles quite differently, the offspring of the former starting out looking like diminutive versions of their elders, while the latter's little ones are anything but chips off the old beetle.

A BEETLE:
Beetles belong to the insect order Coleoptera, and there are more species in that order—over 300,000—than species of anything else on earth.

Unlike bugs, beetles really do chew, and some beetles have mandibles (jaws) so big they could easily take a good chew out of you.

Beetle wings—the uppermost pair, that is—are uniformly thick from base to tip and almost always meet neatly to form a straight line right down the middle of the beetle's back.

And what emerges from a beetle egg is hardly a marvelous miniature; rather than marvelous, what's begotten is larvalous. Like a butterfly, a beetle begins its life as a less-than-lovely larva. The beetle larva (sometimes called, for good reasons, a grub) then turns into a pupa, which in turn metamorphoses to become a much-more-becoming adult.

In-name-only bugs, it's worth noting, commonly have their common names spelled solid—lightningbug, lady-bug, Junebug, etc. Bona fide bugs, however, usually have the names usually used for them split in two—bed bug, stink bug, assassin bug, and so on. The same rule holds true for in-fact and phony flies. Which makes it easier to tell true bugs and flies from bogus ones on the printed page than out in the wild.

A Sweet Potato, A Yam

It's uncanny how you can't find a yam what am a yam inside a can that says it's a can of yams.

A SWEET POTATO:
What actually is inside every mislabeled yam can. A sweet potato is a *root*—the tuber*like* root of *Ipomoea batatas,* a vine that's a member of the morning glory family. Native to the American tropics and now grown in the United States as far north as New England, the sweet potato was once a staple of the ancient Aztec diet.

A YAM:
Unlike the sweet potato, not a root but a true *tuber* (the enlarged tip of an underground stem). There are several species, native to various tropical localities. Consumed mainly by livestock, most U.S. yams hail from Florida. One species, *Dioscorea alata,* grown from the South Sea Islands to India, can produce tubers that are eight feet long and weigh up to 100 pounds. (Cram one of those in a can if you can!)

Two members of the plant kingdom could hardly be classified farther apart. In the class Magnoliopsida, order Solanales, and family Convolvulacaea, sweet potatoes are more closely related to avocados, watermelons, roses, and blueberries than to yams. On the other hand, plants closer to the yams—class Lilaitae, order Liliales, family Dioscoreaceae—than the sweet potato is include asparagus, wheat, orchids, coconuts, bananas, and bamboo.

A Co-op(erative),
A Condo(minium)

Someone trying to sell you a piece of a piece of real estate that doesn't quite feel like a real piece of a piece of real real estate?

A CO-OP(ERATIVE):
A unit in a multiunit apartment building that a corporation that owns the building owns that is leased by the corporation to an individual who owns a piece of the corporation. Honest. (The building itself is also called a co-op or cooperative.) In other words, you own part of a corporation that owns the whole building, and the corporation rents part of the building equal to your part of the corporation back to you. Honest. This makes you, in effect, your own tenant and at the same time your own landlord. Being your own grandparent is only slightly more difficult.

A CONDO(MINIUM):
A unit in a multiunit apartment building that an individual actually owns—lock, stock (but not stock in any corporation), and peephole—individually, along with a shared ownership of the building's site and an interest in the hallways, heating plant, elevators, and other shared facilities. The term also applies to the edifice. While it may be way up high in the sky, a condo doesn't seem so much like pie in the sky, since owning one isn't all that much different, as apartment owning goes, from owning a more traditional terra-firma-planted home.

Photographic Memory, Total Recall

Photographic memory is not just another name for total recall . . . and don't you forget it!

PHOTOGRAPHIC MEMORY:
Just another name for eidetic memory (a.k.a. eidetic imagery). Individuals with photographic memory, sometimes called *eidetikers,* are able to recall images they have previously been exposed to with a vividness that borders on actual visual perception. "Eidetikers," explains *The ABC of Psychology,* edited by Leonard Kristal, "experience these [eidetic] images as if 'seeing' them with extraordinary clarity and detail 'projected' on a wall or screen in front of them; they can examine and describe them in meticulous detail."

Photographic memory in adults is quite rare, but some psychologists estimate that as many as 60% of all children under 12 have picture-perfect memory to some degree. An even less common mnemonic phenomenon is a form of eidetic memory that involves the very clear rehearing of sounds. Sounds like that ought to be called phonographic memory.

TOTAL RECALL:
Simply a really remarkable memory. You might even say memorable. Forget it—make that downright unforgettable. For individuals with total recall, remembering things is a snap, but that's about as close to being photographic as it gets.

Think you can remember that?

A First Edition,
A First Issue

We'll make book you don't know which comes first.

A FIRST EDITION:
According to the first edition of *The Dictionary of Publishing* by David M. Brownstone and Irene M. Frank, a first edition is "the entire original run of copies" of a book "from the same plates, which may be in one printing or in several printings, possibly with corrections in some printings."

A FIRST ISSUE:
"The original press run, or first printing, of the first edition," say Brownstone and Frank, "is called the *first issue* or *first impression*."

Don't forget, you heard it here first.

A Monk, a Friar

One of them begs to differ.

A MONK:
A clerical position in the Roman Catholic Church. The first monks—the Benedictines—appeared on the early Christian scene in the sixth century, and then quickly went into seclusion to pray, bake little round loaves of bread, and go into the liqueur business. Monks lead monastic lives and live in monasteries, which seems only fitting.

A FRIAR:
A clerical position in the Roman Catholic Church similar to a monk. Friars, who first appeared in the thirteenth century, don't hole up in monasteries; they get out and do things. The groups friars belong to—such as the Dominicans, the Franciscans, and the Carmelites—are called mendicant orders, which means that one of the things friars get out and do is beg. Not *all* friars beg, though. Some join up with bands of merry men to redistribute wealth more fairly. When things get too hot in the forest, a friar might hole up in a friary for a while.

Printers know the difference. In print-shop slang, an unwanted smudge or blotch of ink on a printed page is called a *monk*. And an area of ink missing from a page due to improper inking of the printing plate is called a *friar*. The printer's devil must make them do it.

Arbitration, Conciliation, Mediation

It's about time these terms got together to settle their differences.

ARBITRATION:
In between-labor-and-management relations, according to *Robert's Dictionary of Industrial Relations,* arbitration is "a procedure whereby parties unable to agree on a solution to a problem indicate their willingness to be bound by the decision of a third party. The parties usually agree, in advance, on the issues which the third party (the arbitrator) is to decide. This agreement is usually known as the 'submission.' " Even though the parties involved submit to being bound, arbitration is usually not the least bit kinky.

There are all kinds of arbitration. In *ad hoc arbitration,* for example, "the arbitrator is appointed for a single case," whereas in *permanent arbitration* "permanent arbitrators are named in the contract." A "third party dispute settlement required by law—state or federal" is called *compulsory arbitration,* which should not be confused with *obligatory arbitration,* "arbitration which results from the voluntary agreement of parties under a collective bargaining agreement to submit future disputes under the terms of the contract to a third party for settlement." And *voluntary arbitration,* a "third party settlement where labor and management mutually request that an issue be submitted to arbitration," is a far cry from *arbitration under duress,* "an agreement entered into by labor and management to submit a dispute to a third party for final and binding decision, [with] one of the parties [having done so] involuntarily," the pressure having come "from the press, public opinion, or governmental agency."

If two parties can't agree on the kind of arbitration they need an arbitrator for, they can always call on a third party to make the decision.

CONCILIATION:
"In conciliation," according to *Robert's,* "the person acting as conciliator merely attempts to bring parties together to act by themselves in resolving their problems."

MEDIATION:
"In mediation," quoting *Robert's* again, "the involvement of the third party is more active and the mediator attempts to suggest to the parties various proposals and methods for the actual resolution of the problem. In neither conciliation nor mediation does the conciliator or mediator make decisions."

The distinction between mediation and arbitration is today much less clear-cut than it used to be, so which term you now choose to use is pretty much arbitrary.

Disposable Income, Discretionary Income

A whole lot happens to the money you earn before it turns into money to burn.

DISPOSABLE INCOME:
Loophole loot. Also called *surplus income*, it's what cash you have left after paying all your taxes (income taxes, property taxes, gift taxes, Social Security taxes, and so on) and whatever elso your government can get you for, such as traffic fines, public school tuition, auto license fees, and on and on. Disposable income is quite simply what you have left to live quite simply on. Sales taxes, by the way, are very clever taxes designed to tax your after-tax disposable income as you dispose of it.

DISCRETIONARY INCOME:
Mad money. (Which, if you haven't got any, may be defined as money that makes you angry by its absence.) Also called *excess income*, it's what's left over after you pay for rent, food, clothes, utilities, insurance, medical expenses, and all of life's other not-so-little necessities. Discretionary income is money in the bank that can ac-

tually stay in the bank—or be taken out and invested, or squandered on vacations, hobbies, entertainment, luxuries, and vices. These, in fact, are the fabled funds that finance all evil. So, do exercise a little discretion.

Cement, Concrete

People always seem to be mixing them up.

CEMENT:
Concrete it's not. Take a sidewalk survey, though, and ask what's underfoot, and you'll quickly see just how many folks think that it is. Cement is only an ingredient, albeit quite an important one, just one of several that go into making what cement is only a part of and certainly not another name for: concrete.

While there are all kinds of cement, the most common by far is called *portland* (because it looks so much like the stones quarried on an English isle of that name) *cement*. To make it, take some limestone and clay. Grind them up, then mix them together. Heat them in a kiln to around 1300° C until they turn into balls called clinker. Put the cooled-down clinker in another grinder and add some gypsum to grind with it. What you wind up with is portland cement.

CONCRETE:
Cement + water + fine aggregate (sand) + coarse aggregate (gravel) = concrete.

What turns a dirty, wet mush into a mighty, solid mass is what happens when the cement in a mixture of concrete "dries." The cement's anhydrous (waterless) compounds created during the clinkering process react chemically with the water, thereby using it up, turning into H_2O-bound compounds called hydrates—tricalcium aluminate, for example, becomes tetracalcium aluminate—that have tremendous adhesive and cohesive properties (the better to bond fine and coarse aggregates with) and minute crystalline structures that give concrete its great strength and hardness.

What's even harder, however, is figuring out why so many people are so insistent on calling concrete cement. What, for example, does absolutely everyone call those unbuoyant boots made by pouring wet cement and aggregate around an errant underworld underling's trembling underpinnings? Cement overshoes! What else? "Concrete overshoes" admittedly doesn't have quite the same ring. What about "gangland galoshes"?

A Wind, a Draft

You don't want anyone saying you don't know which way the whatever is blowing.

A WIND:
In the great outdoors, a current of air that is moving horizontally. To find out which way the wind is blowing, wet a finger and hold it straight up; the side that gets cold first should be facing the wind.

A DRAFT:
In the great outdoors, a current of air that is moving vertically. There are updrafts (blowing up) and downdrafts (blowing down). To find out which way a draft is blowing, wet a finger and hold it out horizontally.

Upwind and downwind should not be confused with updrafts and downdrafts. Upwind and downwind are terms used to describe the direction the wind is blowing with respect to two different points of reference. Downwind, for example, is where you want to be with respect to a grizzly bear if you are in its vicinity. If you're upwind of a grizzly bear and happen to have an umbrella handy, open it up and pray for one heck of an updraft.

Compost, Mulch

To appreciate the difference takes a good sense of humus.

COMPOST:
Partly decomposed organic material that is spread on top of or tilled into soil to fertilize it and to replenish its humus. Humus, created by the decay of vegetable and animal matter, is the organic component of soil and that part that supplies a large portion of the nutrients needed for plant growth. A to-be-decomposed compost heap is composed of alternating layers of manure (vegetable or animal—yes, there's such a thing as vegetable manure), soil, and various plant materials such as grass clippings, leaves, vegetable trimmings, organic garbage, weeds, and the like. Chemical fertilizers and minerals may be added to the pile to reinforce the compost and hasten decomposition. Kept moist and properly aerated by periodic turning, the compost is gradually transformed by bacterial action into a heap of ready-for-spreading, fertilizer-packed humus.

MULCH:
Any loose material—usually organic but not necessarily—that is placed as a covering over soil for all sorts of beneficial reasons. Leaves, straw, wood chips, torn paper and even plastic can be mixed up in a mulch. Mulch keeps the soil moist by retarding evaporation. A cover of mulch inhibits erosion, increases percolation of water into the soil, and protects plant roots from freezing. Mulchless gardens require much more weeding. There is obviously much to be said for mulch.

Spread on top of topsoil, compost can act just like a mulch, and a mulch that's biodegradable will decompose in time and do much the same thing a compost does. This compost-cum-mulching and mulch-cum-composting just might be the root of all the confusion.

Midnight, December 31, 1999; The Turn of the 21st Century

Order a carload of every color of confetti. Stock up on horns, whistles, and funny hats. Blow up balloons till you're positively blue in the face. Go out and buy a bottle of the very best champagne you can find. Get a magnum. No, a jeroboam. What the heck, make it a methuselah or two. But . . .

MIDNIGHT, DECEMBER 31, 1999:
. . . don't do anything with any of that stuff yet. This isn't it. It's not the big one. It's only the beginning of the very *last* year of what has been one pretty incredible century.

THE TURN OF THE TWENTY-FIRST CENTURY:
midnight, December 31, 2000. This is really it. And well worth the wait. After all, this just might be the last turn of the century ever.

Spumoni, Tortoni

Guess which one comes in a little white cup.

SPUMONI:
It isn't spumoni. Spumoni is the Italian ice cream with the stripes—those little multilayered and multicolored and multiflavored ice cream bricks with bits of fruit and nuts and sometimes candy mixed in.

TORTONI:
And it's not tortoni. Tortoni, named for a famed 19th-century Parisian restaurateur of obvious extraction, is a frozen mousselike dessert made from eggs and heavy cream and frequently laced with cherry bits and topped with minced almonds or crumbled macaroons. Belissimo, grazie, and yum yum, Monsieur Tortoni.

If you wanted your tortoni served in a little white cup, you should have asked for *biscuit tortoni*.

A Cougar,
A Mountain Lion,
A Puma

Most cats have nine lives, but not many have ten names.

A COUGAR:
See *a mountain lion.*

A MOUNTAIN LION:
See *a puma.*

A PUMA:
Scientifically labeled variously *Felis concolor, Puma concolor,* and *Panthera concolor,* and, in addition to puma, commonly called mountain lion, cougar, panther, painter, American lion, and catamount. They're all the same feline—a cat with the largest natural range of any wild cat in the world, stretching from British Columbia in Canada to Patagonia at the bottom of South America, where it no doubt goes by quite a few additional names along the way. Trimming it down to just one scientific name would be helpful. How about *Alias concolor?*

The Redwood, The Giant Redwood

In terms of size they run rings around other trees, but of the two which would you guess is the taller?

THE REDWOOD:
An evergreen conifer, *Sequoia sempervirens*, the tallest of all the trees, and, for that matter, the tallest living anything living anywhere. Also called the California redwood or the coast redwood, each appellation being equally apt, since redwoods grow naturally only along the coast of California. A height of 385 feet was recorded for the all-time-record redwood.

THE GIANT REDWOOD:
The King Kong of conifers, the most massive evergreen you've ever seen, *Sequoiandendron giganteum*, the largest of all the trees, and the largest living anything, in fact, anywhere. Also called the giant sequoia or, simply (and understandably if you've ever stood under a stand of them), the big tree. Like the redwood, it is a native of California, living higher up, though, and farther inland, on the western slopes of the Sierra Nevadas.

The biggest extant examples of these biggest of trees may have sprouted from the ground around 3,500 years ago, measures more than 100 feet around, and can weigh up to 6,000 *tons*. One particularly venerable and voluminous harvested giant redwood yielded a far-from-just-run-of-the-mill 600,000+ board feet of wood. A really tall regular redwood, however, is still taller than even the tallest of giant redwoods, which might not top out at much more than a mere 320 feet.

An Optician,
An Optometrist,
An Ophthalmologist

Now let's raise our glasses high to some men and
women of true vision:

AN OPTICIAN:
Basically, a grinder of lenses according to a prescription. Besides grinding lenses, an optician can fit and measure frames, adjust glasses, and sell them from an office or shop. An optician may *not* examine eyes, prescribe or dispense any medications, or—goodness gracious—perform any sort of surgery. Opticians are licensed and usually study for two years to learn their craft.

AN OPTOMETRIST:
A licensed examiner of eyes and writer of lens prescriptions. An optometrist can also do anything an optician can do, including operating a store that sells glasses, although most optometrists leave the lens grinding to opticians or optical supply houses, which employ opticians. An optometrist can examine for certain muscular dysfunctions of the eye—crossed eyes, for example—and prescribe corrective exercises for them. But dispensing medication (except for eyedrops in some states), treating eye diseases, or performing any kind of surgery is out. Optometrists can test for glaucoma, but they must refer patients they find to have the disease to an ophthalmologist. An optometrist is a doctor, but not a medical doctor. He or she must finish four years of premed training in college and then spend another four years in a college of optometry before receiving an O.D.—Doctor of Optometrics—degree.

AN OPHTHALMOLOGIST:
A licensed medical doctor who specializes in treating the eye and who by virtue of his or her training can treat diseases and disorders of the eye both medically and surgically. An ophthalmologist can also do anything an

optometrist can do, but an ophthalmologist who grinds lenses is rare. Ophthalmologists go to college for four years, medical school for four years, and then spend three more years in a residency in ophthalmology. Some study a little longer, learning how to spell and pronounce their occupation. Those who fail in this last endeavor call themselves oculists.

Is that clear? Read the bottom line again—this time with your hand over your left eye.

A Jet Engine,
A Rocket Engine

Why a jet taking off is always more breathtaking than
a rocket blasting off:

A JET ENGINE:
A reaction engine (an engine whose thrust is created as
a result of the reaction to the ejection of a stream of gas
or liquid from it) that obtains from the surrounding atmosphere the oxygen needed for the combustion of its
fuel. Jet engines are therefore sometimes referred to as
air-swallowing engines.

A ROCKET ENGINE:
A reaction engine that carries with it, in addition to a
chemical or liquid fuel, an oxidizer for combustion,
which permits it to create thrust independent of atmospheric oxygen. Rocket engines can therefore operate in
space, whereas jet engines cannot. Jet engines *and*
rocket engines, since they are both reaction engines, are
by definition propelled by jet propulsion.

That's pretty much the thrust of it.

Chow Mein,
Lo Mein,
Chop Suey

Only one of them has
two things in common with
Rice-A-Roni.

CHOW MEIN:
According to Gloria Bley Miller's *The Thousand Recipe Chinese Cookbook,* "Chow Mein, or 'fried noodles,' is a casual dish which calls for parboiled noodles (previously drained dry and chilled) to be cooked with other ingredients, somewhat in the manner of fried rice; that is, the noodles and other ingredients are fried separately, then combined and cooked briefly together just before serving. The noodles are soft-fried first in oil, then removed from the pan. Next, the various meats and vegetables are stir-fried separately until nearly done. (These, used in various combinations, include: pork, beef, chicken, duck, ham, shrimp, and such vegetables as bamboo shoots, bean sprouts, celery, Chinese cabbage, Chinese lettuce, cucumber, mushrooms, scallions, spinach, and water chestnuts.) The soft-fried noodles are then returned at the end only to reheat and blend flavors."

LO MEIN:

According to *The Thousand Recipe Chinese Cookbook,* "Lo Mein means 'tossed or mixed noodles' and calls for parboiled noodles (also previously drained dry and chilled) to be added, not to the hot oil and soft-fried as in Chow Mein, but directly to the meat and vegetable combinations, which have already been stir-fried. These noodles, tossed or mixed and heated through with the cooked combinations, are moister, having more of a sauce than the Chow Mein."

CHOP SUEY:

A San Francisco treat. An Oriental concoction with Occidental roots you won't find a recipe for in *The Thousand Recipe Chinese Cookbook.* According to *Webster's Third New International Dictionary,* though, the name is Cantonese Chinese and means "odds and ends," from "*shap* miscellaneous + *sui* bits," and it's "a dish prepared chiefly from bean sprouts, bamboo shoots, water chestnuts, onions, mushrooms, and meat or fish and served with rice and soy sauce."

Some say it's far from authentic Chinese fare. But is that really fair? Who cooked it up, we ask? Hungarians? Always start with wonton soup. Have an egg roll on the side. Hold the chopsticks (in other words, use a fork).

And don't forget your fortune cookie.

A Marsh, a Bog,
A Swamp

Squish, squush, squash.

A MARSH:
Squish. A wetland (which is any kind of land where the natural level of ground water is usually or frequently above, at or near the surface) where woody plants, such as trees and shrubs, don't grow but where herbaceous (nonwoody) vegetation—grasses, sedges, rushes, water lilies, etc.—abounds. Low-lying, poorly drained, grassy-growth-supporting areas along rivers are called *freshwater marshes*. Marshes bordering the sea whose wetness waxes and wanes with the tide are called *tidal marshes*.

A BOG:
Squuish. A spongy wetland (with or without a scattering of shrubs and evergreen trees) with a covering of acidy, soft, waterlogged mats of decaying and decayed moss and other vegetation, usually with deposits of peat—incompletely decayed, partially carbonized plant residues—built up and building up beneath.

A SWAMP:
Squash. A wetland that's more wet than land, more woodsy than weedy, and not mossy enough for peat's sake. More or less (more than a marsh or a bog, at least) a bona fide body of water—one supporting an assortment of surface-breaking plants that always includes trees. When the trees that dominate a swamp are predominantly cypresses, it's called a *cypress swamp*. When they're mainly mangroves, it's a *mangrove swamp*. However, you won't find many oaks in Okefenokee.

The Coast,
The Shore

Most people simply don't know where to draw the line.

THE COAST:
The seaward limit of the land. The coast is the edge of any land that borders on any body of water. The coast of France (*pardon, la côte*), for example, borders on, in counterclockwise order, the English Channel, the Atlantic Ocean, and the Mediterranean Sea. The width of a particular coast will vary, depending on the lay of the land, from a narrow strip to one that may extend many miles inland. On its seaward side, however, the coast stops abruptly at the *coastline*, which marks that point where the land becomes permanently exposed and is always high and dry.

THE SHORE:
The landward limit of the sea (or any other significant body of water). The shore (or shores) of Lake Michigan, for example, laps (or lap) against the coasts of Wisconsin, Illinois, Indiana, and, but of course, the state of Michigan.

But "the shore" also refers to part of the terra firma: the relatively narrow zone that is alternately covered and exposed by the action of waves and the rise and fall of the *shoreline*, simply the water's edge that migrates in and out (as well as up and down) with the changing level of the tide. This solid but soggy strip in turn has zones of its own. The *foreshore* is that part of the whole shore that is by turns under water and above water due to the normal comings and goings of your average high and low tides. The *backshore*, just beyond the foreshore, is that part of the shore that is only occasionally awash due to an onslaught of storm waves or an exceptionally high tide. Only when the backshore is completely submerged are the shoreline and the coastline the same line.

"The Coast" and Los Angeles are, of course, synonymous.

Weight Lifting, Power Lifting

You really should be better informed in matters of such gravity.

WEIGHT LIFTING:
The sport involving the lifting of a barbell with weights attached to each end in which the three principal lifts executed in competition are the press, the clean and jerk, and the snatch. In the press, the barbell is lifted to the chest and then slowly extended above the head. In the clean and jerk, the weight is lifted to chest height and then, on a signal from a referee, jerked overhead. In the snatch, the lifter lifts the barbell from the floor to the overhead position in a single, uninterrupted motion.

POWER LIFTING:
The sport involving the lifting of a barbell with weights attached to each end in which the three principal lifts executed in competition are the bench press, the squat, and the dead lift. In the bench press, the lifter, lying on his or her back, lifts the barbell off the chest, extending the arms until the elbows lock. In the squat, the lifter, with the barbell resting behind the neck on the back of the shoulders, squats and then stands up straight. In the dead lift, the lifter simply (or with some difficulty) straightens up from a bent-over position and lifts the barbell from the floor to the thighs.

Any dumbbell knows that.

A Storm Surge,
A Tsunami,
A Tidal Wave

Of the three, surprisingly, the tidal wave's the one one should worry the least about, because even at its worst it's nothing more than a big bore.

A STORM SURGE:
Usually, and always incorrectly, called a tidal wave, a storm surge is a rise in the normal level of the sea along a coast due to the effects of a storm. Very strong storm winds blowing uninterruptedly toward land can cause water to "pile up" against the coast, raising the level of the sea. A significant reduction in atmospheric pressure accompanying a severe storm, such as a hurricane, can also cause a rise in sea levels. When strong onshore storm winds combine with especially low atmospheric pressure so that they simultaneously occur in phase with a normally-high or especially-high high tide, the results can be disastrous.

A TSUNAMI:
Usually, and always incorrectly, called a tidal wave, a tsunami is an ocean wave generated by an unusual dis-

turbance of the surface of the sea. Causes include submarine earthquakes, coastal landslides and volcanic eruptions. A tsunami—which is Japanese for "harbor wave"—resulting from the vertical displacement of the ocean floor caused by an undersea quake is also called a *seismic sea wave.*

Tsunamis may travel thousands of miles before reaching land, and devastating wave heights of 50 feet and more have been recorded. Fortunately, tsunamis are usually rather unimpressive (complete washouts, you might say), and most go completely unnoticed.

A TIDAL WAVE:
Only rarely called a tidal wave, even though it's the only wave here that warrants the title.

All waves, from ocean waves to radio waves, have crests (the highest point of the wave) and troughs (the lowest point between two crests). When the tide in any particular place is at its highest, what's making the tide in that location high is the crest of a tidal wave. The low tide that follows the high tide is the tidal wave's trough. Two great tidal wave crests—one positioned more or less directly below the tide-generating moon and the other 180° away on the other side of the world—sweep around the globe, one crest inexorably following the other approximately every 12½ hours.

When the crest of a true tidal wave encounters a shallow and narrow river estuary and its outflowing current or a coastal configuration that causes the incoming high tide to overtake the outgoing low tide, an observable tidal wave—and a great tourist attraction in some parts—called a *bore* is the result.

The bigger the bore, of course, the bigger the attraction.

Apple Juice,
Apple Cider

Juice? Cider? What's the difference? Not the most pressing question, but one you might be hard-pressed to answer.

APPLE JUICE:
Juice from apples that's more than just pressed juice. It's juice that has also been pasteurized—heated just enough and for just long enough to partially sterilize it—and then hermetically sealed in a bottle or can.

APPLE CIDER:
Just pressed, non-pasteurized apple juice. Let apple cider sit around long enough and its uninhibited, hard-working bacteria will partially ferment it into a drink to which the uninhibited are not impartial: *hard cider*. Hard cider allowed to fully ferment turns into what's called *cider vinegar*—a turn of events some call a shame.

Polygamy, Polygyny, Polyandry

Talk about a wedding march!

POLYGAMY:
Having more than one wife or husband at one time when such a matrimonious condition is harmonious with local laws and customs. When such an arrangement is a nuptial no-no, it's called *bigamy*.

POLYGYNY:
Having more than one legal wife at one time. King Mongut of Siam (the king of *The King and I*) is said to have had 9,000 wives. Mongut, who was a Buddhist monk for 27 years before becoming king of what is now called Thailand, holds the world's record for polygynous marriages . . . and also for making up for lost time.

POLYANDRY:
Having more than one legal husband at one time. Kahena, queen of the Berbers, is also the all-time reigning queen of polyandry. She had 400 husbands. It's not clear, though, whether she spent any time in a convent.

Sashimi, Sushi

Almost everyone knows that one is raw fish, but hardly anyone can tell you which is which.

SASHIMI:
This is the raw fish. Specifically, *sliced* raw fish. Delish. More specifically, sliced *maguro* (tuna), *suzuki* (sea bass), *saba* (mackerel), *makajiki* (swordfish), *anogo* (eel), *swabi* (abalone) and *ika* (squid), among others; garnished with finely chopped or thinly sliced *daikon* (giant white radish), carrot, cabbage, seaweed, and such; customarily eaten with chopsticks and dipped in soy sauce to which a dollop of *watanabi* (powdered Japanese green radish mixed with water) and sometimes other seasonings have been added.

SUSHI:
"Su" in Japanese means vinegar, and the one ingredient common to all the many forms of sushi is vinegared rice.
One popular type of sushi is *nigiri-zushi,* essentially a shaped lump of *shari* (vinegared sushi rice) topped with raw or cooked fish, egg, meat, and sometimes vegeta-

bles. Another sushi favorite is *nori-maki* (seaweed roll), made by rolling up vinegared rice and one or more additional ingredients in a thin sheet of *nori* (dried and toasted seaweed) and then cutting the roll into bite-sized slices that look exactly like little insulated transatlantic cable sections. Mmmmmmmm! A very fat seaweed roll cram-packed with lots of different exotic goodies—sort of a Dagwood sandwich à la Nippon—is called *futomaki*.

Like sashimi, sushi is served (at home or in sushi shops that also dispense sashimi) with a soy-sauce-base dipping solution, but sushi may be eaten with chopsticks or with the fingers, and sashimi is frequently served as a first course before sushi.

It's so simple, one wonders why there is such confusion. After all, who has any trouble remembering the difference between teriyaki and sukiyaki?

A Spire, a Steeple

Here's the church
And here's the steeple.
Open the doors
And look at the people.
Those aren't just people,
That's the choir.
And that's not a steeple,
That's a spire.

A SPIRE:
The tall, pointed *roof* of a church tower; an architectural outgrowth of the Middle Ages, when steep roofs frequently terminated the towers of nonreligious buildings in northern Europe. A spire is only a part of a church tower, not the whole blessed thing.

A small spire atop a pinnacle or turret is called a *spirelet*. A small window in a spire, usually put there more to be illuminating to the eye on the outside than to illuminate what the eye might see on the inside, is called a *spire light*.

As inspiring as the thought might be, the word "spire" was not inspired by the word "inspire." "Spire" has its roots in words that refer to plant shoots and blades of grass that taper to a point, while "inspire" comes from the Latin *spirer*, to breathe or take a breath. A nice coincidence, though, since so many spires are so breathtaking.

A STEEPLE:

The tower *plus* the spire. Or even a tall church tower that isn't supporting a spire. The steeple became so called simply because of its steepness; "steeple" then gave rise to "steeplechase," originally the term for a cross-country horse race whose finish line was at the base of some distant but visible steeple. Now, isn't that inspiring?

Perfume,
Eau de Parfum,
Eau de Toilette,
Cologne,
Eau de Cologne

Want to learn the essence of what separates these hypnotic concoctions? Concentrate.

PERFUME:
Often called *parfum*. A concentration of fragrant oils in alcohol that usually ranges from around 20% oil in 80% alcohol to about 30% oil in 70% alcohol. An occasional perfume (perhaps for a special occasion) may contain as much as 40% oil, but larger concentrations of some oils will actually lessen the strength of the scent. Because of the amount of oil present, water cannot be added, since the former and the latter hate so to mix.

EAU DE PARFUM:
Never called eau de perfume. Usually just another name for what is more accurately called eau de toilette.

EAU DE TOILETTE:
The second-most concentrated scent, after perfume—usually 10% to 18% oil. To a solution that contains less than 13% oil, water can be added. Sometimes called concentrated cologne.

COLOGNE:
The weakest concentration—a very light splash that's anywhere from 3% to 9% oil. A 5%-oil cologne can be more than 11% water. A common misconception among the unscent-savvy is that eau de toilette is weaker, but the only thing less potent than cologne is the standard 2%-oil-or-less aftershave.

EAU DE COLOGNE:
Just the long way to say cologne.

The percentages mentioned above are only approximations, and there are no regulations or industry guidelines governing what can be called what. There's absolutely nothing, in other words, to prevent a fly-by-nuit perfume packager from slapping a fancy label that says "parfum" on a pint of cheap, waterlogged après-le-shave. Many reputable fragrance makers are frankly incensed and feel the whole situation is malodorous.

A Calculator,
A Computer

Go figure this one out:

A CALCULATOR:
A simple, usually hand-held electronic machine used for calculating. "Calculate," says no less definitive a source than *Webster's Third New International Dictionary,* is "usually preferred in reference to more complex, difficult, and lengthy mathematical processes executed with precision and care."

A COMPUTER:
A supersophisticated and powerful desktop or mainframe electronic machine used for computing. "Compute," according to Webster's, is "used for simpler mathematical processes, especially arithmetic ones, and with less abstruse and problematic questions."

The next generation of data processors, truly "intelligent" machines, will probably have to be called *reckoners.* "Reckon," says Webster's, is "an informal and familiar term" and "usually suggests the simplest arithmetic processes."

An Understudy,
A Stand-by,
An Understander

"Break a leg!"—which is how theater people say "good luck," because saying "good luck" is considered bad luck—isn't exactly a universal show biz expression.

AN UNDERSTUDY:
An actor or actress who learns the part played by another actor or actress in a stage play or musical in order to be prepared to go out there and go on in the understudied role should the actor or actress who normally plays it be unable to perform. Actor's Equity, the union that sees to it that all arrangements between actors and actresses and their employers are equitable, also sees to it that all parts, with the exception of those of stars and bit players, are covered by understudies. An understudy, who usually also has a minor part in the production, is required to be present in the theater during all performances. Understudies who are also cast members receive compensation over and above their normal salary, the amount depending on the number of parts they are understudying and what those parts are. Bit players don't very frequently have understudies. When the star of the show is only a star in terms of the show, though, he or she may have an understudy. When the understudy for such a star says "Break a leg!" to such a star, he or she usually really means it.

A STAND-BY:

An actor or actress who covers a star's role in a stage play or musical, especially when the actor or actress starring in the starring role is a real star. A stand-by is usually an already well-respected and perhaps even well-known performer. Stand-bys are paid considerably more for their potential services than understudies, and they aren't required to hang around the theater; a phone call a half-an-hour before curtain time to see if they have to break a previous engagement so they can go on in place of the star is all their contracts usually require of them. Stand-bys are sometimes confused with standees, members of the audience who have bought a ticket not for a seat but for standing room. When a stand-by goes on for a star, however, the number of standees in the theatre usually goes way down.

AN UNDERSTANDER:
A performer whose position in show business is sometimes misunderstood to be somewhere between an understudy and a stand-by, which is only understandable. An understander's appropriate position, though, is instead somewhere *under* one or more other performers—in a circus. Playing a supporting role in an acrobatic troupe, an understander stands under other members of the troupe and holds them up—with the head, hands, shoulders, feet, a perch, etc.—while they juggle, tumble, and perform other such feats overhead. When someone breaks a leg under these circumstances it is almost never intentionally, and quite frequently it is the result of an unfortunate misunderstanding.

A Matador,
A Toreador,
A Torero

No bull:

A MATADOR:
The star in a bullfight; the member of a team of bullfighters who waves the cape (the *muleta*) and kills the bull by plunging a sword (the *estoque*) between the bull's shoulders, assuming the bull doesn't plunge his horns somewhere into the matador first.

A TOREADOR:
An old term for a bullfighter, but especially one who fights bulls on horseback—no longer used by bullfight fans (*aficionados*) but still very popular with opera fans (*buffs*).

A TORERO:
Any of the bullfighters in the bullring, which usually include the matador, two *picadores* who ride around on blindfolded horses poking the bull with a lance, and three fun fellows called *banderilleros* who run around on foot sticking gayly colored darts into the bull's shoulders.

Olé!

"The Industry,"
"The Business"

In both "the Industry" and "the Business," "the Office" means the William Morris Agency.

"THE INDUSTRY":
What the movie business is called by people in "the Industry" and "the Business."

"THE BUSINESS":
What the television industry is called by people in "the Business" and "the Industry."

A Shlemiel, A Schlimazl

"Shlemiel" has won some currency in the English language; however, "schlimazl," as luck would have it, hasn't.

A SHLEMIEL:
Also spelled schlemiel, schlemihl, or shlemihl, a Yiddish term—from a Hebrew word meaning "good-for-nothing"—for a butter-fingered bungler, an unfortunate misfit, an inept fool, or simply a simpleton.

A SCHLIMAZL:
Also spelled schlimazel or schlemazel, a Yiddish term—from a German word for bad, *schlimm*, and the Hebrew word for luck, *mazel*—for a person plagued with chronic lack of luck. A born loser.

"The classic attempt to discriminate between the two types," explains Leo Rosten's *The Joys of Yiddish*, "runs: 'A *shlemiel* is a man who is always spilling hot soup—down the neck of a *shlimazl*.' " But *The New York Times Everyday Reader's Dictionary of Misunderstood, Misused, Mispronounced Words*, which offers: "schlemiel . . . a poor fool who is always the victim of others" and "schlemazel . . . a particularly stupid and awkward person," seems to have gotten its definitions reversed. The editor wasn't a shlemiel, since he must have known better; at worst he was a schlimazl. The shlemiel was probably the typesetter.

A Voyage,
A Passage

Every single day it gets around 4,000,000 miles farther away, and sometime in the summer of '88 it's going to fly clean out of our solar system . . . but we've still got this funny feeling that Voyager I will be coming back.

A VOYAGE:
There may be more than one way to take a trip by sea, but for such a trip to be a voyage it has to be more than one-way. By definition a round trip, a voyage includes both the outward and homeward legs of a journey by sea (and there's no reason why that shouldn't hold as true for seas of space as for seas of water).

A PASSAGE:
Either the outward or the homeward leg of a journey by sea, or a one-way crossing, or any trip from one port to another. Put together an outward passage and a homeward passage, or any number of passages that eventually bring you back to the port whence you departed, and they add up to a bona fide, if not bon, voyage.

A Catch, a Latch

This is really an open and shut case.

A CATCH:
Any device used for holding shut but not locking light-weight doors that does not use any sort of bolt, bar, rod, or hook and that releases automatically when the door is pulled, pushed, or—as is the case with the magnetic push catch described below—pushed and then pulled.

Commonly encountered catches include: the *ball catch*—a catch whose strike holds a communicating projection or finger by means of the pressure exerted upon it by one or two spring-loaded balls; the *friction catch*—a catch whose strike holds a communicating projection or finger by means of the pressure applied to it by the spreading apart of the strike's flexible sides; the *magnetic catch*—a catch with a magnetic strike that holds a communicating plate made of a material that is attracted by the magnet; the *roller catch*—a catch whose strike holds a communicating projection or finger by means of pressure applied by one or two spring-loaded rollers; the *magnetic push catch*—a magnetic catch with an inward and outward moving strike that alternately retracts and projects by means of springs on successive applications of pressure.

A LATCH:
Any door- or window- or gate-holding but nonlocking device that does its securing by means of a horizontal bar that pivots down to bridge the gap between a door and a jamb, or between two doors or two windows that come together, or between a gate and a gatepost, to engage a retaining strike or "keeper." The latch part is disengaged by means of some sort of simple lift-assisting appendage—usually a handle, thumbpiece, or knob.

Four familiar latch types are: the *bar latch*—a simple knob-for-lifting-equipped pivoting horizontal bar mounted on the outside, or pull side, of a door that drops down into a projecting keeper; the *cupboard turn*—a rustic latch of metal or wood consisting of a knob connected to a rod that communicates on the inside side of a cupboard door with a rotating finger which, when turned down on the inside by means of the knob on the outside, secures the door; the *thumb latch*—a latch whose horizontal, strike-engaging latching bar located on one side of a door is raised for disengagement from the opposite side of the door by means of a pivoting, thumb-activated lifting piece that extends through the door; the *Dutch door quadrant*—a quadrant-shaped latch fastened to the bottom leaf of a Dutch door that pivots around the point where the quadrant's radii converge to engage a strike attached to the upper door leaf so as to fasten the two doors.

Natch.

A Moose, an Elk

An elk is only sometimes a moose.

A MOOSE:
A behemoth among bambis, the largest member (males often weigh in at over 1,800 pounds) of the deer family, Cervidae. The moose is found in most Alaskan and Canadian forests and in many of the northernmost forested regions of the continental United States.

The moose is easily recognized by its massive body, long legs, and elongated, overhanging upper lip, or muzzle, which it uses to strip twigs, leaves, sprouts, and tender shoots from low branches, shrubs, and saplings as it browses* for food. The male moose's spectacular palmate (handlike) antlers can attain a spread of six feet. The female moose never grows antlers. Another distinguishing moose feature is the long, pendulous flap of bearded skin, called a "bell," that hangs from the neck and throat.

The moose's scientific name is *Alces alces*.

AN ELK:
The largest member of the deer family in Europe and Asia, with a range that stretches from Norway and Sweden across Russia to Mongolia.

The elk is easily identified by its massive body, long legs, and elongated, overhanging upper lip, or muzzle, which it uses to strip twigs, leaves, sprouts, and tender shoots from low branches, shrubs, and saplings as it browses* for food. The male elk's spectacular palmate (handlike) antlers can attain a spread of six feet. The

*not to be confused with grazing.

female elk never grows antlers. Another distinguishing elk feature is the long, pendulous flap of bearded skin, called a "bell," that hangs from the neck and throat.

The elk's scientific name? *Alces alces*, if you hadn't already guessed.

The North American moose and the Eurasian elk are both *Alces alces*. Once considered separate species, they are now recognized almost universally as one and the very same animal.

In North America, however, there browses another elk. Its scientific name is *Cervus canadensis*. It isn't a moose. It is closely related to, but not the same animal as, a European deer called the Old World red deer. The North American elk is more correctly called a *wapiti*. Look it up. Under "w."

An Order, A Command

Want your eggs scrambled semisoft, with home fries extra well-done and two slices of dry rye toasted light? Don't just order it. Command it!

AN ORDER:

In the various armed forces, where the only scrambled eggs of any consequence decorate the visors of officers of consequence, an order, according to the *Naval Terms Dictionary* of U.S. Navy Captains J. V. Noel and Edward L. Beach (who are both retired and presumably no longer giving or taking any orders *or* commands), an order "directs that a job be done but does not specify how."

A COMMAND:

An order of a different order, say Noel and Beach, "directing a particular action in a specific way." A directive with directions. Commandments, of course, are orders of the highest order from the Very Highest Authority.

™, ®

Sticks and stones may break your bones, but losing your trademark can put you out of business.

™:

A symbol placed just above and to the right of a trademark (a name, symbol, distinctive phrase, or other identifying device used by a manufacturer or service to distinguish a particular product or service from those of others). ™ is placed there to say to all who see it: "Hands off! This is *my* trademark. I used it first, so that's that!" Being the first to use a trademark automatically protects it, provided the user who used it first can prove it.

®:

A symbol placed next to a trademark in place of ™ that says: "I even went and sent my trademark to the U.S. Patent Office, and now it's on file there, so you *really* better keep your cotton-pickin' hands off it if you know what's good for you!" Registering a trademark in Washington doesn't protect its user any better, but it doesn't hurt to let everyone know that the government knows you have a MONOPOLY*.

*In the place of this asterisk (the one above, that is), there used to be an ®, but the MONOPOLY people, Parker Brothers, recently lost their monopoly on MONOPOLY. They lost a lawsuit, did not pass GO, and did not collect millions of dollars.

A Cyclotron,
A Synchrocyclotron,
A Synchrotron

What these machines do—literally in whiz-bang
fashion—is simply smashing.

A CYCLOTRON:
A machine developed to overcome a problem with the
earlier, linear accelerators used by nuclear physicists to
send positively or negatively charged chunks of atoms
smashing into atom targets to study a whole slew of
quirky atomic minichunks that flew out in all directions
from the collisions. To push their particles faster and
faster, linear accelerators had to get longer and longer.
When the mile mark was passed, physicists started looking to the horizon for a substitute.

The cyclotron was the answer. It saved space in the
long run by sending its charged particles around and
around in an ever-widening circular path between two
slightly separated, facing semicircular chambers that
fast-track particle pushers like to call "dees" because
they resemble the letter D. As a particle crosses the gap
between dees, the polarity of the dees is reversed, giving
the crossing particle an accelerating kick. Magnets above
and below force the particle into a circular path back

toward the gap and another kick. With each kick, the particle picks up speed and its path spirals wider and wider. The time it takes for each trip around a dee, however, doesn't change, because the increase in the distance traveled is compensated for by the increase in speed. The frequency of the oscillating accelerating voltage, therefore, never has to be changed, which physicists agree is one of the nicest features of the cyclotron.

By the time the accelerated particle reaches the widest possible path—after having made maybe millions of revolutions and traveled perhaps hundreds of thousands of miles—its speed is enormous and it is ready to be directed into an appropriate target.

A SYNCHROCYCLOTRON:

A machine developed to overcome one of the problems with the cyclotron.

Particles accelerated by a cyclotron can go just so fast before something funny happens to them. As they approach the speed of light (approximately 186,000 miles per second) their mass increases—just as Albert Einstein had predicted in his Theory of Relativity—which causes them to slow down just enough to throw the cyclotron's harmonious distance-speed-frequency arrangement out of phase. As a result, the spiraling particle doesn't get its kick at exactly the right time, which only gums up the works.

The synchrocyclotron, or *phasotron*, solves this problem by modulating the frequency of the accelerating voltage, decreasing it to keep in step with the particle as it grows increasingly ponderous.

A SYNCHROTRON:

A machine developed to overcome one of the drawbacks of the synchrocyclotron.

The design of the synchrocyclotron calls for magnets of enormous size, sometimes weighing many thousands of tons. A synchrotron uses lots of smaller magnets situated around a tube that is curved into the shape of a doughnut that in some machines is over a mile in diameter. Focused by the magnets to keep them from spiraling outward as they speed up, particles are accelerated around and around through the tube in an orbit with a constant radius.

The cyclosynchrotron? No doubt they're working on it.

Speed, Velocity

This is going to be quick:

SPEED:
The distance an object travels during a unit of time.

VELOCITY:
The distance an object travels *in a specified direction* during a unit of time.

Next.

A Gorge,
A Canyon

"Isn't that gorge just grand!"

"I'll say. And isn't that canyon just gorge!"

A GORGE:
"A valley that is a little open at the top," writes Professor Otto Franzle in *The Encyclopedia of Geomorphology*, "its transverse profile resembling a very narrow V, is called a gorge. Gorges can only originate in resistant rocks. In regions of high elevation, they may be hundreds or even thousands of feet deep."

A CANYON:
"A V-shaped valley cut into nearly horizontal strata of unequal resistance is characterized by a step-like profile, where the exposed edges of the more-resistant strata form the sheer rises and some of the benches; those of the lesser-resistant strata form the intervening slopes. This special variant of the gorge is called a canyon. . . . The most magnificent of its kind is the Grand Canyon in Arizona, cut through more than 4000 feet of nearly horizontal sedimentary strata and more than 1000 feet into the underlying crystalline rock."

Some geologists dispute this distinction, saying gorges are the same as canyons and canyons are just gorges, and "canyon" is what all gorges are called way out West. But what do you suppose that steep-walled, 1000-foot-plus gash is cutting straight down through the Grand Canyon's underlying resistant crystalline rock? Why, even the most hard-headed geologists admit deep down that it's different—and call it without resistance the "inner gorge."

One Helluva Snowstorm, A Blizzard

The Blizzard of '88, the blizzard to end all blizzards, wasn't a blizzard.

ONE HELLUVA SNOWSTORM:
The Blizzard of '88—which raged from March 11 to March 14, 1888, dropped 40 inches of snow, or better, over southeastern New York State and southern New England, recorded average winds of 20 to 25 miles per hour (with gusts that reached 50 to 70 miles per hour), and caused over 400 deaths (200 in New York City alone, along with over 20 million 1888 dollars in damage) was one helluva snowstorm. But it wasn't a blizzard.

A BLIZZARD:
The elements of weather necessary for a full-blown blizzard, says the U.S. Weather Bureau, are: *sustained* winds of 35 miles per hour or more; temperatures of 20°F or lower; and falling and/or blowing snow (it doesn't even have to be snowing) sufficient to reduce visibility to less than 500 feet. Gusts, says the Weather Bureau, just don't count. So, the big snow of '88 was simply too slow a blow. And it was far from what the Weather Bu-

reau calls a *severe blizzard:* sustained winds of *45* miles per hour, temperatures of 10°F or lower, and enough snow snowing and/or blowing to bring visibility right down to absolute *zero*.

Oh well, there's always March *1*988.

A Cyclone,
A Tornado

Uncle Henry and Aunt Em had a big bed in one corner and Dorothy a little bed in another corner. There was no garret at all, and no cellar—except a small hole, dug in the ground, called a cyclone cellar, where the family could go in case one of those great whirlwinds arose, mighty enough to crush any building in its path.

A CYCLONE:
A 50-or-so-to-2,000-or-more-mile-wide weather system characterized by air circulating about a region of low atmospheric pressure, and usually nothing to send you running underground—unless that's where you stow your umbrella. In fact, below ground or even on low ground just might be the worst of all places for sitting out the worst of all possible cyclones.

The rotation of the earth is what sends the winds that converge on a cyclone's low-pressure center circling about it, counterclockwise in the Northern Hemisphere and clockwise in the Southern Hemisphere. And what determines the speed of a particular cyclone's winds is a combination of things, including the difference between the pressure inside the cyclone and the pressure of the air surrounding it and the distances between the intervening zones of pressure.

The widest cyclones, and the mildest in terms of winds, happen mostly in the temperate middle latitudes in both hemispheres. Caused by warm tropical air masses invading cold polar air masses, these *extratropi-*

cal cyclones move from west to east at around 20 to 30 miles per hour, often travel for thousands of miles over land and sea before dissipating, and are the major makers of meteorological mayhem—lousy weather, in other words, to anyone who isn't a farmer or a bumbershoot baron. (The fair weather that inevitably follows foul is a rather anticlimactic—if not anticlimatic—feature of reversely revolving, high-pressure *anticyclones*.)

Not-so-wide-measured-side-to-side (between 100 and 300 miles ordinarily) cyclones born over tropical oceans make up for their relative lack of size in their wildness. Driven by the heat liberated by the very water it condenses into its enormous clouds and torrential rains, such a cyclone, called a *tropical cyclone*, can generate 130-mile-per-hour winds, but only has to get them up to 75 to qualify as a full-blown *hurricane*. And the extreme low pressure at the center of such a storm can literally lift up tides (see "Tidal Wave, Storm Surge, Tsunami"), which is reason enough to head into the hills, or in the direction of any other handy higher ground.

> *From the far north they heard a low wail of the wind, and Uncle Henry and Dorothy could see where the long grass bowed into waves before the coming storm. There now came a sharp whistling in the air from the south, and as they turned their eyes that way they saw ripples in the grass coming from that direction also.*

A TORNADO:
A whiz of a wind if ever a whizzing wind there was.

Like a cyclone's, a tornado's winds rotate counter-clockwise above the equator and in the opposite direction below it—at an amazing rate some estimates say exceeds 400 miles per hour. And what the winds of a tornado, or *twister*, whiz about in a fearsome funnel is also a center of low atmospheric pressure—so low, in fact, that it can cause even well-built buildings to blow themselves apart from the force of their own relatively high internal pressures.

But a tornado isn't a maker of miserable weather, only an uncommon result of it—a rare product of a thunderstorm, which itelf is one of the not-so-rare products of a true cyclone. Descending from cumulonimbus clouds when atmospheric conditions are conducive, tornadoes skip across the landscape in a dance of destruction that, fortunately, normally covers no more than a few country miles and usually lasts no longer than an hour. And tornadoes' widths, thank goodness, are measured in yards rather than in hundreds of miles. Can you imagine a real cyclone-size one, say, 2,000 miles wide? Why, everything everywhere would end up in Oz!

> *Suddenly Uncle Henry stood up.*
> *"There's a cyclone coming, Em," he called to his wife; "I'll go look after the stock." Then he ran toward the sheds where the cows and horses were kept.*
> *Aunt Em dropped her work and came to the door. One glance told her of the danger close at hand.*
> *"Quick, Dorothy!" she screamed; "run for the cellar!"*
> *—The Wizard of Oz*

A Bit, a Byte, A Nibble

Shave and a haircut . . .

A BIT:
In short (and long, as a "*b*inary dig*it*"), the most miniscule niblit of information any digital computer's innards can digest. The on-again-off-again (yes–no, plus–minus, 0–1, "she/he loves me"–"he/she loves me not") relationship between bits are the basic ingredients in the binary notations computers have such an appetite for.

A BYTE:
Eight bits.
    Computers munch bits not one (one one or one none, that is) by one but in bunches—in equal-size informational forkfuls. And some computers, quite logically, including most micro-sized personal computers, find just one byte just right for a meaningful mouthful. More powerful minicomputers and some two-fisted micros, though, pack in two bytes (16 bits) at a time.

A NIBBLE:
As much of a morsel as some daintier data processors are programmed to peck away at. Just half a byte, a hardly filling four bits.

. . . half a nibble.

A Hue, a Shade, A Tone, a Tint

All the colors of the rainbow . . .

A HUE:
The quality possessed by any color that makes it possible for us to call that color green, red, bluish green, yellowish green, yellowish blue, brown, brownish pink, yellow, reddish orange, and so on. The hue of a color (which is tantamount to saying "the *color* of a color") is what distinguishes it—irrespective of its lightness or darkness or brilliance or whatever—from all the other colors in light's visible spectrum, which is what a rainbow displays on a misty day and what colors separated out of a beam of "white" light that has passed through a prism make.

. . . and then some.

A SHADE:

A color variation having to do with the *value* of a hue, which is a measure of its relative lightness or darkness. The term is sometimes specifically employed to specify a decidedly darker version of a given hue; if, however, you should say, say, "I think I'd like to try several different shades" of this or that color, then that's a value judgment that could easily go either way.

A TONE:

A color variation with more variations than a shade, having to do with the value of a hue *or* its chroma (saturation, or purity) *or* any combination of the two. A hue with a relatively high (light) value and a relatively high (pure) chroma will produce a tone that's positively "brilliant." Combine the same high value with a chroma that's low (less saturated) and you'll wind up with a tone that's "pale" by comparison. Low value and high chroma make a tone "deep," while a hue with low value and low chroma in tone terms is downright "dark."

A TINT:

A color variation that usually refers to any hue's lighter side, used almost exclusively with respect to colors high in lightness and low in chroma and therefore relatively pale and frail.

An Oral Agreement, A Verbal Agreement

They're the same when they're the same and they're not when they're not—and we'll put that in writing.

AN ORAL AGREEMENT:
An agreement that is spoken. An oral agreement may also be called a verbal agreement.

A VERBAL AGREEMENT:
An agreement that is written *or* spoken. Any agreement involving words, either written or spoken, is a verbal agreement. A verbal agreement that is spoken is also an oral agreement. However, a verbal agreement that is written should never be called an oral agreement.

Don't you agree? Say you do. Or write.

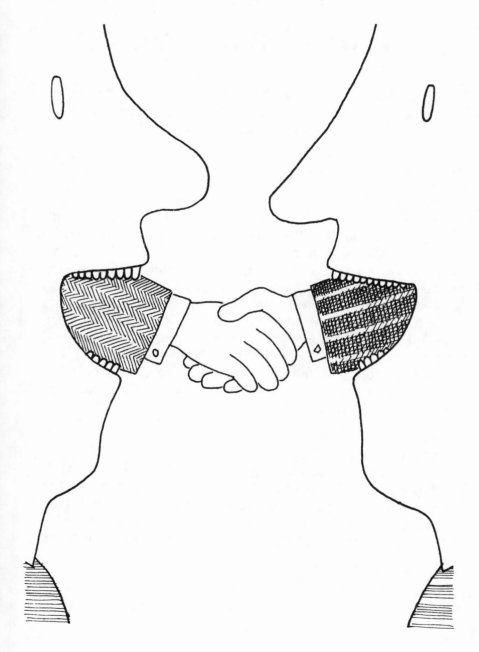

The Middle Ages,
The Dark Ages

The Middle Ages and the Dark Ages are no longer considered the same, and still thinking they are is considered positively medieval.

THE MIDDLE AGES:
The period in European history that began with an ending (the final fall of the Roman Empire) and ended with a beginning (the Italian Renaissance) and filled the gap between the ancient world and the modern with, among other things, those well-known days of olde when legendary knights were so bolde. Actually three ages within one—the Early Middle Ages (A.D. 476 to 900 or 1000), the High Middle Ages (900 or 1000 to around 1300), and the Late Middle Ages (1300 to 1500)—it spanned a far-from-middling millenium, which is twice as much history as the history that has passed since the Middle Ages passed into history.

THE DARK AGES:
What Renaissance men and women called all of the Middle Ages, in keeping with their very dim view of the proceedings of the era immediately preceding them. Historians today, however, if they use the term at all, use it only when referring to the Early Middle Ages, because

the 500 or so years after A.D. 1000, these enlightened scholars now agree, wasn't actually such a bleak period. After all, the only memorable events that might not have recommended it were The Hundred Years War, the ill-fated Children's Crusade, The Spanish Inquisition, and the Great Plague, which wiped out only around half the entire population.

The Atlantic Provinces, The Maritime Provinces

The question is, which is greater—the number of people who don't know *what* they are, or the number of people who don't know *where* they are?

THE ATLANTIC PROVINCES:
Canada's four easternmost provinces: New Brunswick; Nova Scotia (which isn't, no matter how many people think it is, an island); Prince Edward Island (which obviously *is* an island); and Newfoundland (which consists of the island of Newfoundland (the world's sixteenth-largest) and a more-than-twice-the-size-of-the-island chunk of the mainland called Labrador). When Canada was confederated in 1867, Nova Scotia and New Brunswick signed up right away. Prince Edward Island joined six years later. Newfoundland played hard to get all the way up to 1949.

THE MARITIME PROVINCES:
Just New Brunswick, Nova Scotia, and Prince Edward Island, the three provinces that before 1867 were united as a separate political entity.

Where the Maritime Provinces (a.k.a. the Maritimes) and the greater Atlantic Provinces are on the map is not, as maybe even more people than think Nova Scotia's an island seem to believe, just a snowball's throw from the North Pole. Labrador, the northernmost part of the Atlantic Provinces, isn't any farther north than the British Isles. And Halifax, the capital of Nova Scotia, is, believe it or not, a bit farther south than Venice.

Clairvoyance, Precognition, Telepathy

Back in 1934 he dubbed them all ESP, and he could easily tell one from another, but then again Professor Joseph B. Rhine of Duke University was a very, very perceptive fellow.

CLAIRVOYANCE:
What the message from the medium is often the product of. Meaning "clear seeing," this form of ESP (extrasensory perception) may be defined as the supernormal ability to perceive objects or events located or taking place at too far a distance—some say even clear over to that so-called and so-spooky "other side"—to be perceived through the normal sense channels.

The clairvoyance variants are many. Communicating with spirits is called *platform clairvoyance*. *X-ray clairvoyance* is more down-to-earth and permits the "percipient" to, for example, peruse someone else's mail without having to breach the seal on the envelope. A relatively common but still fairly far-out form, *traveling clairvoyance,* involves out-of-body mental trips to witness distant scenes.

PRECOGNITION:
"Before knowing." Seeing into the future. The supernormal ability to know what is going to happen before it happens. (Knowing that a fellow larger than you is going to put a hurting on your nose because you just told him what kind of boots his mother prefers to wear is not a supernormal ability and, therefore, not precognition.) Things "foreseen" by means of precognition are called *premonitions*. Premonitions often lead to *predictions*. And predictions can lead to a job writing for *The National Enquirer*.

Some scientific investigators consider precognition a branch of clairvoyance and call it *previsional clairvoyance*. This may or may not be confirmed by the results of future research, but you would think precognosticators could find out all about those findings right now if they only put their minds to it.

TELEPATHY:
Mind reading. Thought transference. Mind-to-mind communication between two individuals with no dependence on the normal senses. The one form of ESP in which two heads are unquestionably better than one.

If you have a strange feeling you've read all of this before, it may have something to do with any one or all of the above.

A Dove, a Pigeon

Lovebirds they're not, but they're closer than you might think.

A DOVE:
Any bird of the family Columbidae, of which there are approximately 300 species. Smaller species tend to be called doves.

A PIGEON:
Any bird of the family Columbidae, of which there are approximately 300 species. Larger species tend to be called pigeons.

Lovebirds are parrots. Put a lovebird in a cage with a dove—or pigeon—and the last thing you'll hear is billing and cooing.

A Nautical Mile, A Knot

Don't worry. Your ship will come in. After all, it is sailing along at a mile a minute.

A NAUTICAL MILE:
Just a minute . . . of latitude, that is. Also called a geological mile or an Admiralty mile.

Because our less-than-perfect world is slightly flattened on top and bottom (an oblate spheroid, should anyone ever ask), a minute of latitude doesn't measure the same at the equator (6045.93 feet) as it does at the poles (6107.98 feet). So, for practical purposes of navigation, most practical navigators have settled on an in-between distance of 6080 feet.

The other mile, called either the land mile or the statute mile, measures 5280 feet. To convert nautical miles to statute miles, multiply by 38, then divide by 33. To convert statute miles to nautical miles, multiply by 33 and then divide by 38. Either way, it only takes a minute.

A KNOT:
The unit used for measuring nautical miles—in terms of *speed*, that is, not distance. Knots, in other words, measure how fast a vessel is moving in nautical miles per hour.

Savvy salts figured out a long time ago that if you tied knots 47 feet, 3 inches apart in a rope, tossed the end overboard, then counted the number of knots that ran out in the space of 28 seconds, the number of knots counted would equal the number of nautical miles your ship would travel at that speed within the space of an hour. If, say, ten knots ran out in the 28 seconds, you could count on your vessel covering ten nautical miles in an hour. A sailor truly worth his salt, though, would say his ship was "*making* 10 knots."

Because the knot is so closely tied to the nautical mile, it's no wonder so many landlubbers misuse it as a measure of distance. Now that you know it's not, let's just hope that ship of yours isn't sailing off like 60 in the wrong direction.

A Woodcut,
A Wood Engraving

A woodcut can be quite nice, but wouldn't you really rather have a Bewick?

A WOODCUT:

The very first prints on paper—dating back to the beginning of the fifteenth century, when paper first became a common commodity—were woodcuts.

Making a woodcut is a relief process. Knives and gouges of varying size are used to cut into a block of wood, with the grain, to remove wood that corresponds to the negative parts of the design and leave on the surface, or in relief, the positive image to be transferred. The block is then inked. Paper is applied and rubbed down with a burnisher, spoon, or similar tool. When the paper is peeled from the block, the ink image is taken with it. Woodcuts using more than one color usually call for separate blocks, one for each color.

The first two great masters of the woodcut were Albrecht Dürer and Hans Holbein the Younger. Both created major works around the turn of the sixteenth century, and both frowned on being called "woodcutters," which in Germany is what you call someone who runs off into the woods to chop down trees.

A WOOD ENGRAVING:
Late in the eighteenth century, nearly 400 years after the advent of the woodcut and at a time when there was paper aplenty, British engraver and illustrator Thomas Bewick (pronounced like the car) cut *across* the grain with tools he usually used for engraving on metal, printed the block in relief as one would a normal woodcut, and thereby invented wood engraving.

The printed image of a wood engraving is usually composed of fine white lines against a black background—just the reverse of what a normal woodcut would usually look like. Wood engraving became a very popular technique for illustrating books, but toward the end of the nineteenth century the photographic halftone process did to the wood engraving what the word processing process promises to do soon to the typewriter.

An Egoist, an Egotist, A Narcissist

If you're one, you probably know you're one. And you just love it!

AN EGOIST:
Someone who thinks the whole wide world revolves around that selfsame very special someone.

AN EGOTIST:
Someone who just can't stop talking in the most glowing terms just about that selfsame very special someone.

A NARCISSIST:
Someone who is head over heels in love with that self-same very special someone—whatever that special someone's special character defects might be.

Ah, but *you*, of course, already knew all that.

A Muskmelon,
A Cantaloupe

Next time you shop for a cantaloupe, don't just buy a nice one—buy a *real* one.

A MUSKMELON:
Any of several fruits produced on the vines of one of the many different varieties of the plant *Cucumus melo,* which belongs to the gourd family. Some botanists call all *Cucumus melo* melons muskmelons, while others divide them up into muskmelons, Persian melons, casaba melons, honeydew melons, and cantaloupes. The sometimes separated-out muskmelon, *Cucumus melo reticulatus,* has a netted skin; big ones usually come to market as muskmelons and little ones are customarily called cantaloupes.

A CANTALOUPE:
Cucumus melo cantalupensis, the true cantaloupe, which is rarely seen among melons marketed in America. It has a hard shell and a smooth skin, is grown almost exclusively in the Mediterranean countries, and is very popular all over Europe—but especially in Cantalupo, Italy.

A Finishing Nail,
A Brad

They're both common nails that aren't common
nails, but that's not all they both do and don't have
in common.

A FINISHING NAIL:
Unlike most other nails (which have large, circular, flat
heads), a finishing nail has a very narrow head shaped
like a small ball flattened off at the end. Finishing nails
are made that way so they can be countersunk—driven
out of sight below the surface of the wood.

A BRAD:
A countersinkable nail with nearly no head at all, and
usually shorter than a finishing nail.

It's not a big distinction, but we thought we'd drive the
point home anyway.

Entomology, Etymology

en • to • mol • o • gy \entə ' mäləje, -ji\ *n* [F *en-tomologie,* fr. Gk *entomon* insect (fr. neut. of *entomos* cut up, cut in, fr. *entemnein* to cut in, cut up, fr. *en-* ²en- + *temnein* to cut) + F -*logie* -logy—more at TOME] 1 : zoology that deals with insects 2 : a treatise on insects.

—Webster's Third New
International Dictionary

ENTOMOLOGY:
See definitions 1 and 2 above.

ETYMOLOGY:
What's in the brackets in the definition above.